Ready-to-
Independent Reading
Management Kit

by Beverley Jones and Maureen Lodge

SCHOLASTIC
PROFESSIONAL BOOKS

New York ■ Toronto ■ London ■ Auckland ■ Sydney ■ Mexico City ■ New Delhi ■ Hong Kong

Dedication

We would like to thank our students who have taught us and continue to teach us.

Beverley Jones
Maureen Lodge

Edited by Linda Ward Beech

Cover design by Judy Kamilar

Cover photograph © Robert Finken/Photo Researchers

Interior design by Ellen Matlach Hassell
for Boultinghouse & Boultinghouse, Inc.

Cover and interior illustrations by Steve Cox, with additional illustrations on pages 19 and 33 by James Graham Hale and pages 33, 34, and 100 by Rusty Fletcher

ISBN: 0-439-04238-0

Contents

Level 8

Level 9

Level 10

Additional Reproducible Forms

Introduction

The *Ready-to-Use Independent Reading Management Kit* was born out of the need for reading and writing activities that meet the diverse levels of learners in the primary classroom. Our solution was to develop independent reading contracts, which are a series of activity packs that can be used with any book.

For each contract, children make choices about which reading, writing, and skill-building activities they will complete. Making choices fosters a sense of responsibility and ownership, encouraging children to take the contracts seriously. This program helps students learn to select appropriate books, organize the materials they need, and work independently on meaningful and structured activities that help them get the most out of their reading experiences. The program also allows teachers to work with one group of students while the rest work independently on their contracts.

There are ten different contracts in this book that range in complexity from Level 1 to Level 10. Each contract is organized into different areas of activities. Level 1 contains two categories: reading and writing. Levels 2 and 3 include reading, writing, and skills.

Within the skills category, you'll find activities relating to phonics, punctuation, vocabulary, and parts of speech. Levels 4 through 10 include art as a fourth category. More than 80 of the activities come with appealing, illustrated reproducible sheets to help kids stay on task. They'll write a letter of advice to a character, design a travel brochure based on the setting, go on a punctuation hunt, and much, much more!

The various levels of the contracts, the variety of activities within each one, and the flexibility to use the contracts with any book will help you meet the needs of all your learners. The section entitled How to Use This Book on pages 6–8 will take you through the process step by step, from helping students learn to select books to assessing their work. At the end of the book, you'll find other useful reproducible materials, including a letter home explaining the program, a self-assessment rubric, a blank contract, and more. We think that you will find independent reading contracts to be a valuable tool for classroom management and for enriching reading, writing, and language arts. Happy reading!

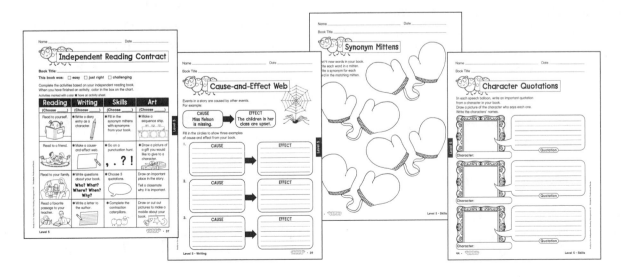

How to Use This Book

Setting Up the System

To meet the needs of all your learners, collect a variety of levels of books for your classroom library. These books can be from your own collection, the school or public library, or donations from families.

Store the books by level in boxes or on shelves to help children make selections easily. We have found that it is helpful to create a center with books, independent reading contracts, copies of the activity pages, and any necessary supplies. To help children work independently, show them where everything is kept and how to put away materials when they are finished using them.

For each column on the contract, you will find a space to fill in the number of activities you want students to complete. This can be determined by the amount of time you want to spend on the contract or by the particular areas you want to focus on. It is also an opportunity to modify the assignment for individual students, if necessary. After filling in the number of activities for each column, make a copy of the contract for each student.

In advance, determine how long you would like students to spend on each contract level. We have found that two to three weeks is usually a good amount of time. Every child works at a different rate, but you can set a time frame within which children can work. As the contracts progress in difficulty, they require more time.

If a student finishes a contract for one book, he or she can complete a contract of the same level for a new book if time permits. Set aside a few blocks of time each week for children to work on their contracts. Once students are comfortable with the procedures, they can work independently while you meet with individuals or small groups. This is also a good time to have conferences with students who have completed a contract. (See Completing a Contract, on page 8.)

Student Selection of Literature

To introduce independent reading contracts in your classroom, begin by demonstrating how to choose a book that is "just right" for the reader. For example, you might pose these questions for children to use:

- Can I read most of the words?
- What is this book about?
- Does the subject interest me?
- Can I read the book without much help?

By showing books that are too easy, too difficult, and finally just right, you can set an example of appropriate book selection.

> *Teacher Tip* You might also teach children the "hand test" strategy to use when they are choosing a book.
> 1. Open to the middle of the book.
> 2. Hold up one hand and open it so your fingers are straight.
> 3. Read a page of the book.
> 4. Each time you come to a word you don't know, bend one finger down.
> 5. If you finish the page and one finger is still up, the book is probably the right level for you.

Introducing New Skills

Before introducing an independent reading contract, look it over to note the skills that children need to complete it. For instance, before beginning the Level 1 contract, children need to know how to write a complete sentence. One or two weeks before introducing the contract, conduct mini-lessons to introduce the skill. Students will then practice that skill as they complete the contract.

When introducing skills such as verbs, compound words, or contractions, you may want to make a poster with examples of these words on it. Students can then refer to the poster if their book selection does not include a good variety of these types of words. In our classroom, students have also enjoyed adding to the posters as they come across "poster words" in their books.

> ***Teacher Tip*** Many of the contracts give students the choice to read to someone at home. This is a great way to get family members involved in students' learning experiences. Communicate with parents and other caregivers about independent reading contracts at the beginning of the school year. Send home the reproducible letter on page 111 or explain the program at a Parents' Night meeting.

Starting an Independent Reading Contract

Once children have selected their books, model how to use an independent reading contract. Start by reading a story aloud to students. Make an overhead transparency of the Level 1 contract sheet. After reading the story, show students the Level 1 contract. Fill in the name, date, and book title lines and check the reading level: easy, just right, or challenging. Explain that each student will fill in this information and complete the activities based on his or her own independent reading book.

Point out that the first column on a contract lists reading activities. Students should always begin by doing the first activity in the reading column, which is to read a part of the book to themselves. Draw attention to the second box in the reading column: Read to a classmate. With a student, role-play appropriate ways to ask a classmate to listen and to reply to a reading invitation. Demonstrate an appropriate reading volume so that students will not disturb their classmates.

Explain that as children complete each activity, they should color in the corresponding box on the contract. Then they should choose their next activity. Point out the number of activities per column that students should complete. Explain that after children complete the reading activities, they can do the activities in the other columns in any order they wish.

Draw children's attention to the asterisk in the corner of the boxes on the contract and explain that this means there is a reproducible page on which to complete the activity. Show children where they can find these activity pages. (It is helpful to keep the activity pages for each contract in a labeled folder.) Demonstrate the procedures children should follow for activities that do not have reproducible sheets. Show students where to find materials, as well as how to use them and put them away. For example, children will need basic art supplies for many of the activities in the art column. You may wish to set up an art center for this purpose.

Throughout the year, continue to model procedures to reinforce and ensure the quality of both the work and the working environment.

Storing Work in Progress

Completing an independent reading contract may take a couple of weeks. It is important to help children organize their materials so that they can work effectively on their own. Have students store all of their materials for their current contract in a pocket folder, including their book. It is helpful for students to staple their contract to the inside left of their folder for easy reference. Designate a place for students to keep their folders, such as in their desks, cubbies, or a file-folder box.

Meeting the Needs of Your Students

There are a variety of ways you can use independent reading contracts to meet your students' range of needs. Each contract level works with any book of any reading level. The contracts build in complexity from Level 1 to Level 10. Students are progressively given more activities to choose from; they are also asked to write more and to use higher levels of critical thinking. As students move to higher-level contracts, you can ask them to complete more activities in each column.

We have found that it works best to have all students work on the same level contract at the same time. The reading level of the books that children choose and the number of books that they read tailor the program to each child's needs. We set aside a three-week period for children to work on one contract level. During this time, a student may complete activities for one book while another student may complete activities for three books. It simplifies the process to have students work at the same level so that you can set up materials and plan mini-lessons geared toward that contract level. Use the blank independent reading contract on page 112 to create additional contracts that reflect skills you would like to reinforce.

Completing a Contract

When a student completes an independent reading contract, he or she is ready to "check out." Show students how to fill in the check-out form on page 108. Also show students how to fill out a self-assessment rubric on page 109 when they have completed a contract. You may wish to model this procedure by evaluating sample work that you have created. Have students staple all of their work in order along with the contract, the rubric, and the check-out form on top. Students should put all of this into a folder and turn in their work at a designated spot. (This could be a basket on your desk or a file-folder box in a reading center.) Periodically check to see that students have finished their contracts so that you can schedule a conference with them. During conferences you can help students evaluate their work using the assessment rubric. You can keep a record of each student's work throughout the year by using the reproducible Teacher Record on page 110.

If a student has completed a contract and if time permits, a student may choose a new

Teacher Tip To keep an ongoing record of students' oral reading skills, set up an audio recording station in your classroom. If possible, invite parent volunteers to help students record themselves throughout the year reading passages from their books. Write a short note explaining that the audio recording is of the student reading. Photocopy the note and send it home to parents along with the tapes in resealable plastic bags.

book and complete another contract at the same level. Students can use the same contract for several different books because the responses for each book will be different. Children can keep a record of the books they have read by filling in the chart on page 107.

Moving On to New Contracts

When your class has mastered the skills on a contract, they are ready to progress to the next level. We have found that students are ready to move on to a new level contract every three weeks. We recommend discussing and modeling the use of each contract as you introduce it. This is also a good opportunity to discuss any issues that arise about procedures, materials, behavior, and performance.

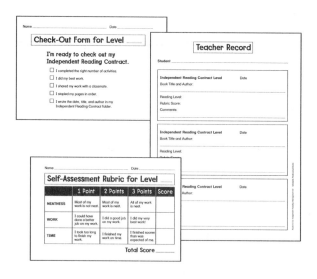

Name _____ Date _____

Independent Reading Contract

Book Title: _____

This book was: ☐ easy ☐ just right ☐ challenging

Complete the activities based on your independent reading book.
When you have finished an activity, color in the box on the chart.

Activities marked with a star ✴ have an activity sheet.

Reading	Writing
(Choose _____)	**(Choose _____)**
Read to yourself.	✴ Copy a super sentence from your book.
Read to a friend.	✴ Make 4 fishy word cards with new words from your book.
Read to your teacher.	✴ Describe the main character.

Name _____   Date _____

Book Title _____

Super Sentence

Copy a super sentence from your book.

_____

_____

_____

_____

_____

In the box, draw a picture to illustrate the sentence.

Ready-to-Use Independent Reading Management Kit   Scholastic Professional Books

Fishy Word Cards

In your book, find 4 words you don't know.
Write each word on a card.
Look up the word in the dictionary and write the meaning on the lines.

Cut out each card.
Write your name on the back of each card.

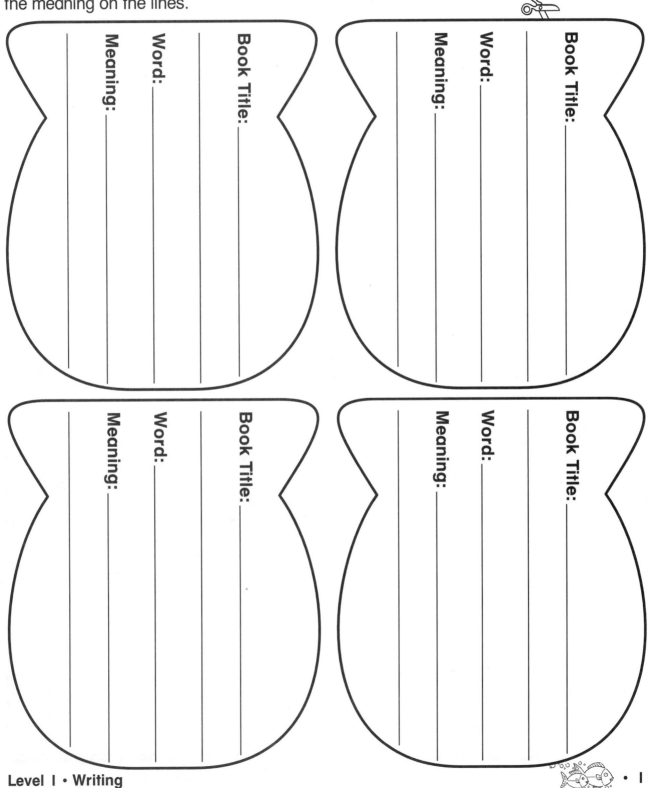

Book Title:

Word:

Meaning:

Book Title:

Word:

Meaning:

Book Title:

Word:

Meaning:

Book Title:

Word:

Meaning:

Ready-to-Use Independent Reading Management Kit   Scholastic Professional Books

Name _____ Date _____

Book Title _____

Describe the Main Character

Write a few sentences
describing the main character.

_____

- -

_____

- -

_____

In the box, draw a picture of the main character.

```




```

Ready-to-Use Independent Reading Management Kit   Scholastic Professional Books

Name _____ Date _____

Independent Reading Contract

Book Title: _____

This book was: ☐ **easy**   ☐ **just right**   ☐ **challenging**

Complete the activities based on your independent reading book.
When you have finished an activity, color in the box on the chart.

Activities marked with a star ✷ have an activity sheet.

Reading	Writing	Skills
(Choose _____)	**(Choose _____)**	**(Choose _____)**
Read to yourself.	✷What does the title tell you?	✷Find 4 words that you can rhyme with other words. **cat bat** **fall tall** **fun sun**
Read to a friend.	✷Make a shopping list of things a character might buy.	✷Find words that begin with each letter of your name.
Read to your teacher.	✷Describe your favorite part of the book.	✷Find words that contain short-vowel sounds. **a e i** **o u**

Name _____   Date _____

Book Title _____

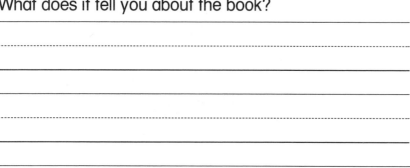

Write a few sentences about the book's title.
What does it tell you about the book?

_____
_____
_____
_____
_____
_____
_____
_____
_____
_____

Draw a picture of the book's cover below.

14 •

 **Level 2 • Writing**

 *Ready-to-Use Independent Reading Management Kit   Scholastic Professional Books*

 **Level 2**

Name _____ Date _____

Book Title _____

Shopping List

Imagine that a character in your book is going to the store.
Make a list of things the character might buy.

_____
- - - - - - - - - - - - - - - - - - -
_____'s

Shopping List

1. _____

2. _____

3. _____

4. _____

5. _____

6. _____

7. _____

8. _____

Ready-to-Use Independent Reading Management Kit Scholastic Professional Books

Name _____ Date _____

Book Title _____

My Favorite Part

My favorite part of the book is

_____

_____

_____

I like this part because

_____

_____

_____

In the box, draw a picture of your favorite part.

Name _____ Date _____

Book Title _____

Rhyme Time

Look in your book for 4 words that
you can rhyme with other words.
Write the words on the left.
Write the rhyming words on the right.
In the boxes, draw a picture for each word.

house

mouse

Words From Book	Words That Rhyme
1.	
2.	
3.	
4.	

Name _____ Date _____

Book Title _____

Name Game

Write your name in the boxes below.
(Write one letter in each box.)
Write a word from your book that
begins with each letter of your name.

B big
R road
E each
N night
D dog
A all

☐ --

☐ --

☐ --

☐ --

☐ --

☐ --

☐ --

☐ --

☐ --

Name _____ Date _____

Book Title _____

Short-Vowel Search

Find 2 words from your book that contain
each of the following short-vowel sounds.

short a

cat

_____   _____

short e

hen

_____   _____

short i

pig

_____   _____

short o

frog

_____   _____

short u

duck

_____   _____

Ready-to-Use Independent Reading Management Kit   Scholastic Professional Books

Level 2 • Skills   **• 19**

Name _____ Date _____

Independent Reading Contract

Book Title: _____

This book was: ☐ **easy**   ☐ **just right**   ☐ **challenging**

Complete the activities based on your independent reading book.
When you have finished an activity, color in the box on the chart.

Activities marked with a star ✱ have an activity sheet.

Reading	Writing	Skills
(Choose _____)	(Choose _____)	(Choose _____)
Read to yourself.	✱ Write a postcard about your book. Dear _____ To: _____	✱ Choose 5 words from your book and put them in ABC order. 1. bag 2. dinner 3. napkin
Read to a friend.	✱ Write 3 questions for a character.	✱ Find 4 compound words. butterfly
Read to your teacher.	✱ Make a plot chart.	✱ Find words that begin with blends. fr

Ready-to-Use Independent Reading Management Kit   Scholastic Professional Books

Name _____ Date _____

Book Title _____

Write a Postcard

Write a postcard to someone who you think would like this book.
Explain why this person would like the book. (Include the title.)
Write the person's address on the lines at right and draw a stamp.
Cut out the postcard.
Draw a picture on the back of the postcard.

✂

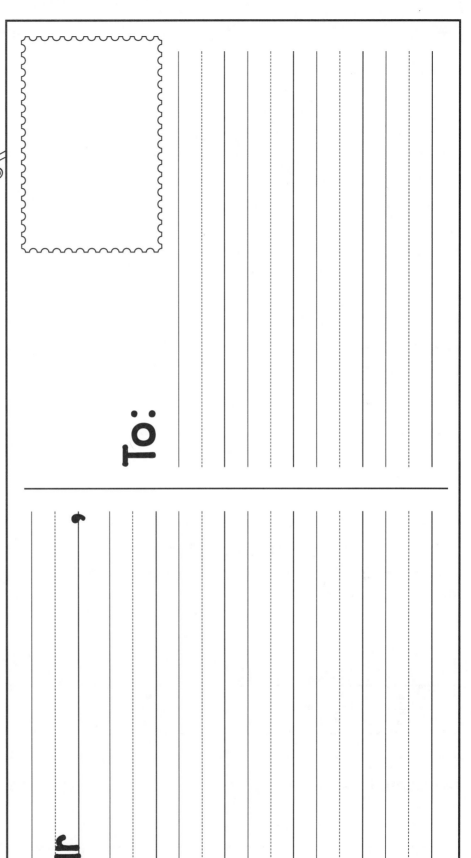

To:

Dear

Name _____ Date _____

Book Title _____

Character Interview

Imagine that you are going to interview a character in the book. Think of 3 questions to ask this character.
Write them on the lines below.

Name of Character
_____
_____

Question 1
_____
_____
_____
_____

Question 2
_____
_____
_____
_____

Question 3
_____
_____
_____
_____

★Bonus★ Think about how the character might respond to your questions.

Ready-to-Use Independent Reading Management Kit Scholastic Professional Books

Name _____ Date _____

Book Title _____

$$\boxed{\textbf{Plot Chart}}$$

A story plot moves from one event to the next.
Fill in the chart to show the main events in your book.

Event 1
_____
- -
_____

Event 2
_____
- -
_____

Event 3
_____
- -
_____

Event 4
_____
- -
_____

Ending of book
_____
- -
_____

Name _____ Date _____

Book Title _____

ABC Order

Choose 5 words from your book.
Write them in ABC order.

1. _____

2. _____

3. _____

4. _____

5. _____

Ready-to-Use Independent Reading Management Kit Scholastic Professional Books

Level 3 • Skills

Name _____ Date _____

Book Title _____

Compound-Word Search

Find 4 compound words in your book.
In the left column, write the compound words.
In the right columns, write the 2 words that form each compound word.
Draw a picture above each word.

Compound Word	Word 1	Word 2
football	foot	ball
1.		
2.		
3.		
4.		

A Bunch of Blends

In your book, look for a word that starts with
each of these blends: *st, fr, cl, pl,* and *sp*.
On the lines, write the words.
In the boxes, draw a picture for each word.

st	
fr	
cl	
pl	
sp	

Ready-to-Use Independent Reading Management Kit   Scholastic Professional Books

Name _____ Date _____

Independent Reading Contract

Book Title: _____

This book was: ☐ **easy** ☐ **just right** ☐ **challenging**

Complete the activities based on your independent reading book.
When you have finished an activity, color in the box on the chart.

Activities marked with a star ✱ have an activity sheet.

Reading	Writing	Skills	Art
(Choose ____)	(Choose ____)	(Choose ____)	(Choose ____)
Read to yourself.	✱ Retell the beginning, middle, and end.	✱ Go on a syllable search.	✱ Design a new cover for your book.
Reread your favorite part.	✱ Write a letter about your book.	✱ Look for long-vowel words in your book. **a e i o u**	Make a paper bag puppet of a character in your book.
Read to a classmate.	✱ Choose a character you would like to be friends with. Explain why.	✱ Do a noun sort.	Draw your favorite place in the story. Tell a classmate why it is your favorite place.
Read to your teacher.	✱ Create an ad for your book.	✱ Find 4 fantastic adjectives and use them in sentences.	Draw an illustration for any part of your book.

Ready-to-Use Independent Reading Management Kit   Scholastic Professional Books

Name _____

Date _____

Book Title _____

Story Sundae

In the ice cream scoops, write about the beginning, middle, and end of the book. Draw an illustration for each part.

Beginning

Middle

End

Ready-to-Use Independent Reading Management Kit   Scholastic Professional Books

Name _____ Date _____

Book Title _____

Pen Pal

Write a letter to someone about your book.
Here are some ideas of what to include in your letter:

✔ the title and author of the book

✔ what your book is about

✔ what you like about the book

✔ if you would recommend the book

_____

_____

                                                  Date

Dear _____ ,

_____

_____

_____

_____

_____

_____

_____

        _____

        _____

        _____

        _____

Ready-to-Use Independent Reading Management Kit   Scholastic Professional Books

Name _____ Date _____

Book Title _____

Friends With a Character

Choose a character that you would like to
be friends with.
Write a short paragraph explaining why.
What do you like about this character?

Name of Character

_____

....

_____

I would like to be friends with this character because . . .

_____
....
_____
....
_____
....
_____
....
_____
....
_____
....
_____
....
_____
....
_____
....

Ready-to-Use Independent Reading Management Kit   Scholastic Professional Books

Name _____ Date _____

Book Title _____

Create an Ad

Create a magazine ad to sell your book.

Include the following in your ad:

- ✔ book title
- ✔ author
- ✔ illustrator
- ✔ what the book is about
- ✔ why the book is good

On a separate sheet of paper, draw a picture to go with your ad.

_____

_____

_____

_____

_____

_____

_____

_____

_____

_____

_____

_____

_____

_____

Name _____

Date _____

Book Title _____

Syllable Search

Find words in your book that have 1, 2, 3, or more than 3 syllables.
List each word under the correct heading on the chart.
Use a dictionary if you need help.

1 syllable	2 syllables	3 syllables	more than 3 syllables
big	hippo	animal	hippopotamus

Name _____ Date _____

Book Title _____

Look for Long Vowels

In your book, look for a word that
has each long-vowel sound in it.
Write the words on the lines.

long *a*   whale   _____

long *e*   tree   _____

long *i*   tiger   _____

long *o*   boat   _____

long *u*   unicorn   _____

Name _____ Date _____

Book Title _____

Noun Sort

Find 15 nouns in your book.
Write 5 nouns under each heading.

Person	Place	Thing
princess	beach	flower

Ready-to-Use Independent Reading Management Kit   Scholastic Professional Books

Name _____ Date _____

Book Title _____

Four Fantastic Adjectives

Find 4 fantastic adjectives in your book.
Write them on the lines.
Use each adjective in your own
descriptive sentence.

Adjective

1.

2.

3.

4.

Sentence

Name _____ Date _____

Book Title _____

Design a New Cover

Design a new cover for your book.
Write the book title on your cover.
Write the names of the author and illustrator.

Ready-to-Use Independent Reading Management Kit   Scholastic Professional Books

Name _____   Date _____

Independent Reading Contract

Book Title: _____

This book was: ☐ easy   ☐ just right   ☐ challenging

Complete the activities based on your independent reading book.
When you have finished an activity, color in the box on the chart.

Activities marked with a star ✱ have an activity sheet.

Reading	Writing	Skills	Art
(Choose _____)	(Choose _____)	(Choose _____)	(Choose _____)
Read to yourself.	✱ Write a diary entry as a character.	✱ Fill in the synonym mittens with synonyms from your book.	✱ Make a sequence ship.
Read to a friend.	✱ Make a cause-and-effect web.	✱ Go on a punctuation hunt. , . ? !	✱ Draw a picture of a gift you would like to give to a character.
Read to your family.	✱ Write questions about your book. **Who? What? Where? When? Why?**	✱ Choose 3 quotations.	Draw an important place in the story. Tell a classmate why it is important.
Read a favorite passage to your teacher.	✱ Write a letter to the author.	✱ Complete the contraction caterpillars.	Draw or cut out pictures to make a mobile about your book.

Name _____ Date _____

Book Title _____

Diary of a Character

Character: _____

Pretend you are a character in the book.
What would the character write in a diary?
Write from the character's point of view
about something important in the book.

<u>Dear Diary,</u> _____

Ready-to-Use Independent Reading Management Kit   Scholastic Professional Books

Name _____ Date _____

Book Title _____

Cause-and-Effect Web

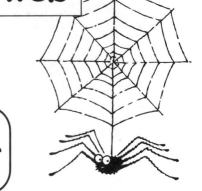

Events in a story are caused by other events.
For example:

CAUSE		EFFECT
CAUSE Miss Nelson is missing.	→	**EFFECT** The children in her class are upset.

Fill in the boxes to show three examples
of cause and effect from your book.

1.

CAUSE		EFFECT
CAUSE	→	**EFFECT**

2.

CAUSE		EFFECT
CAUSE	→	**EFFECT**

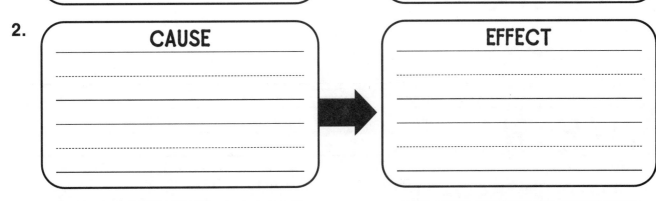

3.

CAUSE		EFFECT
CAUSE	→	**EFFECT**

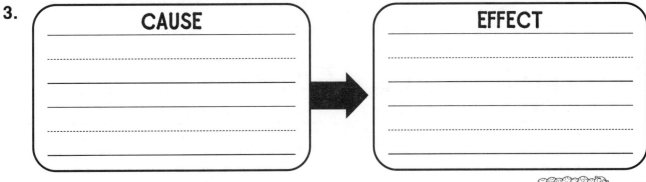

Ready-to-Use Independent Reading Management Kit   Scholastic Professional Books

Name _____   Date _____

Book Title _____

Use each word to begin a question about your book.
Be sure to end your sentences with a question mark.

Who

What

Where

When

Why

Level 5 • Writing

Ready-to-Use Independent Reading Management Kit   Scholastic Professional Books

Level 5

Name _____ Date _____

Book Title _____

 **Dear Author**

Write a letter to the author of your book.
Tell why you liked the book.
Include the book title in your letter.

```
                                    _____
                                    - - - - - - - - - - -
                                    _____
                                              Date
_____


Dear _____ ,
_____
- - - - - - - - - - - - - - - - - - - - - - - - -
_____
- - - - - - - - - - - - - - - - - - - - - - - - -
_____
_____
- - - - - - - - - - - - - - - - - - - - - - - - -
_____
_____
- - - - - - - - - - - - - - - - - - - - - - - - -
_____
                        _____
                        - - - - - - - - - - - - -
                        _____
                        _____
                        - - - - - - - - - - - - -
                        _____
```

Ready-to-Use Independent Reading Management Kit   Scholastic Professional Books

Level 5

Name _____   Date _____

Book Title _____

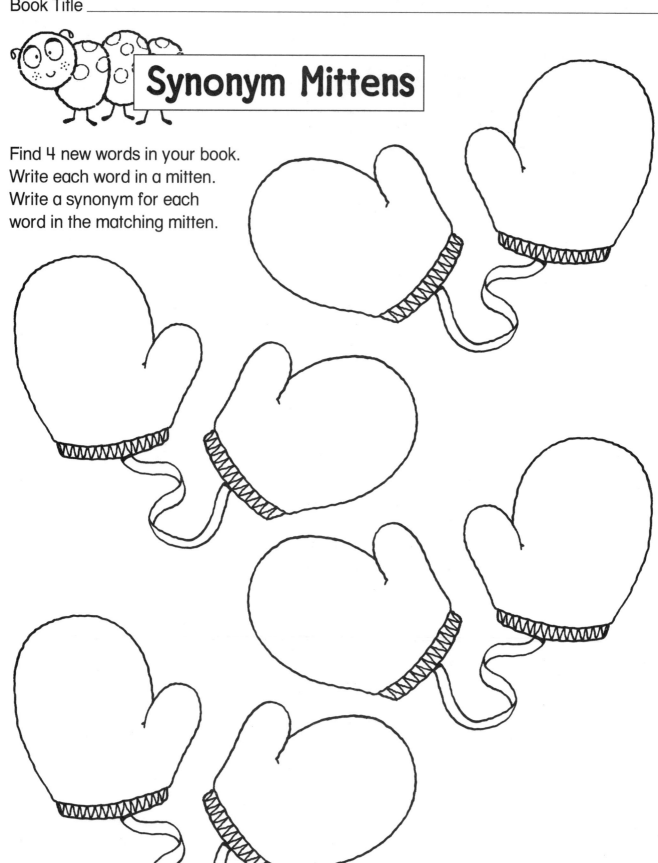

Synonym Mittens

Find 4 new words in your book.
Write each word in a mitten.
Write a synonym for each
word in the matching mitten.

Ready-to-Use Independent Reading Management Kit   Scholastic Professional Books

Name _____ Date _____

Book Title _____

Punctuation Hunt

Look in your book for each kind of sentence.
Write the sentence on the lines.

A sentence ending with a period:

_____
_____
_____
_____

A sentence ending with an exclamation point:

_____
_____
_____
_____

A sentence ending with a question mark:

_____
_____
_____
_____

A sentence with a comma:

_____
_____
_____
_____

Name _____   Date _____

Book Title _____

Character Quotations

In each speech balloon, write an important quotation
from a character in your book.
Draw a picture of the character who says each one.
Write the characters' names.

Quotation

Character:

Quotation

Character:

Quotation

Character:

Ready-to-Use Independent Reading Management Kit   Scholastic Professional Books

Name _____   Date _____

Book Title _____

Contraction Caterpillars

Find 4 contractions in your book.
Write a contraction in each
caterpillar's head.
In the body, write the 2 words
that make up the contraction.
(Write each word in a separate
part of the caterpillar's body.)

it   is   it's

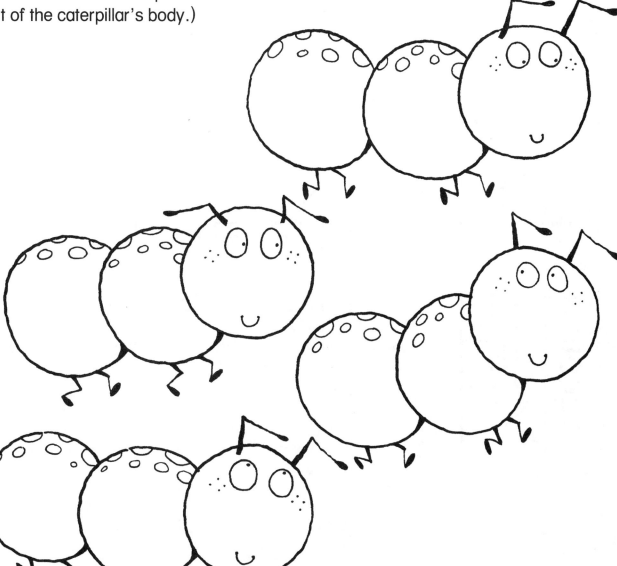

Level 5

Sequence Ship

In each porthole, draw a main event in the story.
Draw the events in the order in which they happen.
On the lines, write about each event.

Name _____

Book Title: _____

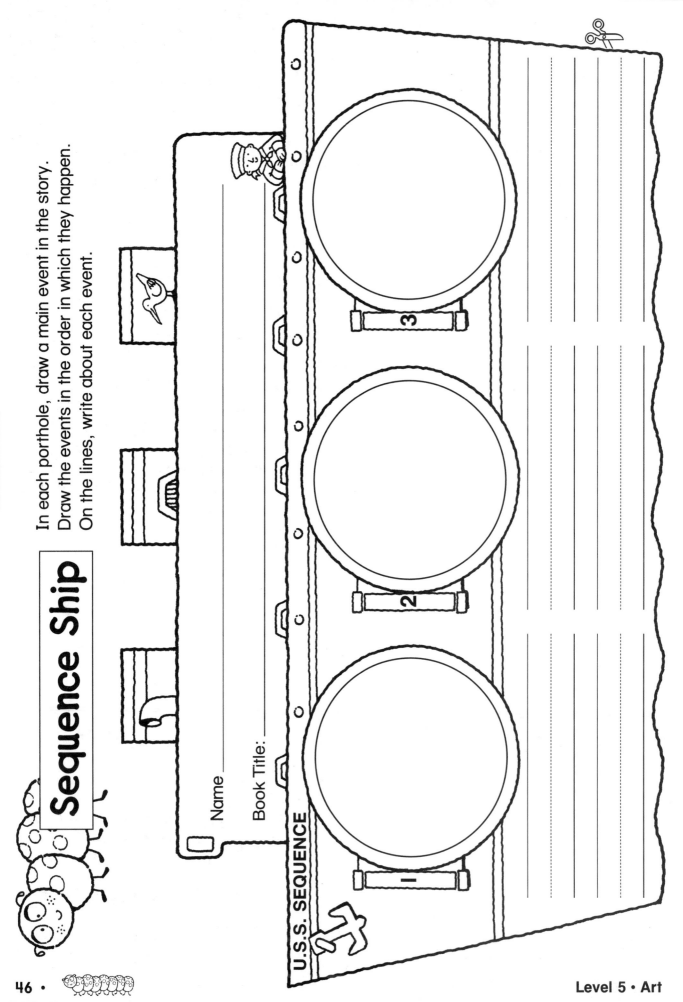

U.S.S. SEQUENCE

46 •

Ready-to-Use Independent Reading Management Kit   Scholastic Professional Books

Draw a Gift

Draw a gift that you would give
to a character in the book.
Fill in the gift tag.

To: _____

From: _____

Name _____ Date _____

Independent Reading Contract

Book Title: _____

This book was: ☐ easy   ☐ just right   ☐ challenging

Complete the activities based on your independent reading book.
When you have finished an activity, color in the box on the chart.

Activities marked with a star ✱ have an activity sheet.

Reading	Writing	Skills	Art
(Choose ____)	(Choose ____)	(Choose ____)	(Choose ____)
Read to yourself.	✱ Make predictions about what will happen in your book.	✱ Make a word search with nouns.	✱ Make a bookmark about your book.
Read to a student in a lower grade.	✱ Write a recipe for your book.	✱ Look for plural nouns in your book. cats	Paste pictures to make a collage about your book.
Read to someone at home.	✱ Research the author of your book.	✱ Go on an action-verb hunt. **ran yell tumble sing**	Make a character mask.
Read to your teacher.	✱ Write a new ending for the book.	✱ Search for silent-*e* words. *sshh!*	Make a poster about your book.

Ready-to-Use Independent Reading Management Kit Scholastic Professional Books

Name _____ Date _____

Book Title _____

I Predict . . .

Fill in the left column of the chart
before you read the book.
Fill in the right column *after* you
read the book.

Before Reading	After Reading
I predict that the book is about:	This is what the book really is about:
I predict that the main character will:	This is what really happens to the main character:

Ready-to-Use Independent Reading Management Kit Scholastic Professional Books

Name _____ Date _____

Book Title _____

Recipe for a Book

What are the ingredients of your book? Fill in the recipe card below.

Recipe for _____
(book title)

From the kitchen of (author) _____

Ingredients (characters) _____

_____ (setting)

Directions (what happens in the book) _____

Ready-to-Use Independent Reading Management Kit   Scholastic Professional Books

Level 6 • Writing

Name _____ Date _____

Book Title _____

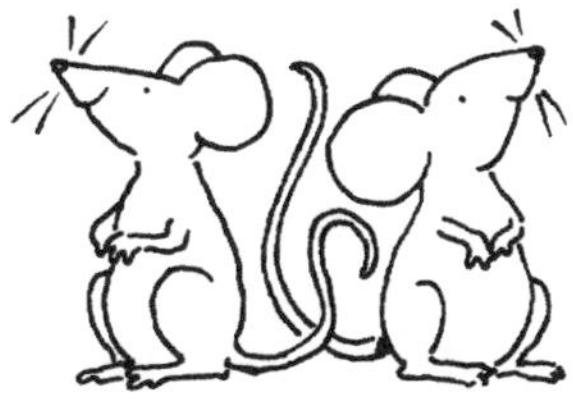

Author Research

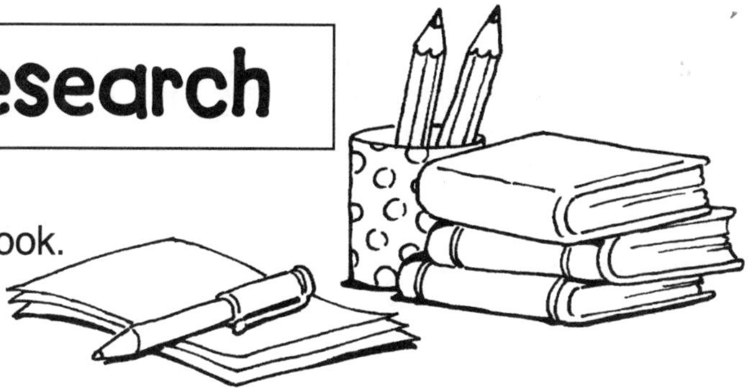

Find information about the author of your book.
Fill in the facts below.

Author:

_____

_____

Where the author is from:

_____

_____

Other books the author has written:

_____

_____

_____

_____

_____

_____

_____

Interesting facts about the author:

A drawing of the author:

_____

_____

_____

_____

_____

_____

_____

_____

_____

_____

Name _____ Date _____

Book Title _____

 | **A New Ending**

Write a new ending for your book.

_____

_____

_____

_____

_____

Draw a picture to go with your ending.

Ready-to-Use Independent Reading Management Kit   Scholastic Professional Books

Wonderful Word Search

Find 5 nouns in your book and list them.
Then write the words in the grid.
(Write one letter in each box.
The words can go across or down.)
Add other letters to the grid to hide the words.
Ask a friend to find and circle the words.

Word List

1. _____

2. _____

3. _____

4. _____

5. _____

Word Search

Level 6

Name _____

Date _____

Book Title _____

Plenty of Plural Nouns

Look for 10 plural nouns in your book.
Write each plural noun under the correct
heading below.

s	es	ies	special plurals
 cats	 dishes	 ponies	 mice

Ready-to-Use Independent Reading Management Kit Scholastic Professional Books

Name _____ Date _____

Book Title _____

Action-Verb Hunt

In your book, find 4 verbs that
show action.
Write a verb on each line.
Draw a picture for each verb.

1. _____

2. _____

3. _____

4. _____

Ready-to-Use Independent Reading Management Kit Scholastic Professional Books

Name _____ Date _____

Book Title _____

Search for Silent-e Words

In your book, look for 5 words that end in silent *e*.
Write them on the lines.

1. _____

2. _____

3. _____

4. _____

5. _____

sshh!

★**Bonus**★   Can you think of any
other words that end in silent *e*?
Write them here.

_____

_____

_____

_____

_____

Ready-to-Use Independent Reading Management Kit   Scholastic Professional Books

Name _____ Date _____

Book Title _____

Make a Bookmark

Cut out the bookmark.
Fold it along the dotted line.
Draw a picture on one side.
Write why you like the book on the other side.

✂

Title:

I like this book because

_____ Fold along dotted line. _____

Ready-to-Use Independent Reading Management Kit Scholastic Professional Books

Name _____   Date _____

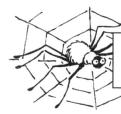

Independent Reading Contract

Book Title: _____

This book was: ☐ **easy**   ☐ **just right**   ☐ **challenging**

Complete the activities based on your independent reading book.
When you have finished an activity, color in the box on the chart.

Activities marked with a star ✱ have an activity sheet.

Reading (Choose ____)	Writing (Choose ____)	Skills (Choose ____)	Art (Choose ____)
Read to yourself.	✱ Make a story web about your book.	✱ Find an adjective for every letter.	✱ Make a mini-book based on your story.
Read to your school librarian.	✱ Write about the problem and solution.	✱ Find verbs with different endings.	✱ Make a puppet of your favorite character.
Read to someone at home.	✱ Make a character cube.	✱ Fill in the antonym ants with words and their antonyms.	Design an award for a character. Write why you gave the character this award.
Read your favorite part to your teacher.	✱ Write a poem about your book.	✱ Use a dictionary to find the meaning of new words.	Make a mosaic of your book's setting. Glue small pieces of colored paper onto another sheet of paper.

Ready-to-Use Independent Reading Management Kit   Scholastic Professional Books

Level 7

Ready-to-Use Independent Reading Management Kit   Scholastic Professional Books

Name _____ Date _____

Book Title _____

Make a Story Web

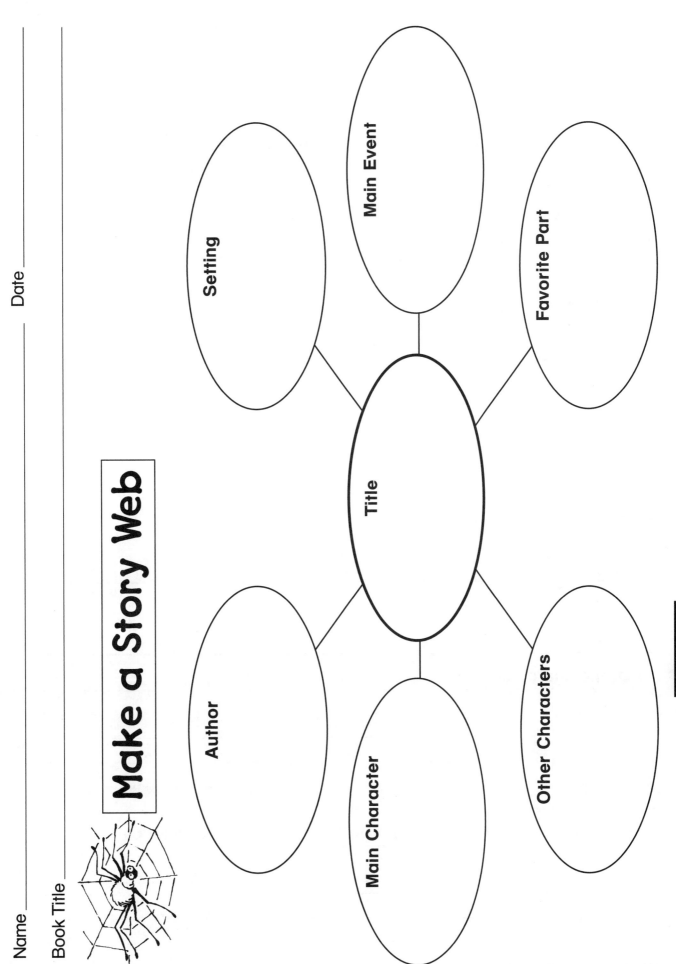

- Setting
- Main Event
- Favorite Part
- Title
- Author
- Main Character
- Other Characters

Level 7

Level 7 • Writing

Name _____ Date _____

Book Title _____

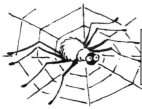

What's the Problem?

The main character in a book almost always
has a problem or a goal.
The solution of the story tells how the character
solves the problem or reaches the goal.
Complete these sentences about the problem
or goal in your book.

The character's problem (or goal) is

_____

_____

_____

_____

First, the character tries

_____

_____

_____

_____

Then, the character

_____

_____

_____

_____

Finally, the character solves the problem or reaches the goal by

_____

_____

_____

_____

Ready-to-Use Independent Reading Management Kit   Scholastic Professional Books

Level 7

Name _____ Date _____

Book Title _____

Character Cube

Cut out the pattern.

Write the character's name and some brief information about him or her.

Fold and glue the pattern into a cube.

Share your cube with a friend.

1. Character's Name

_____

_____

_____

_____

2. Three Words to Tell How the Character Looks

_____

_____

_____

5. Three Words to Tell What the Character Is Like

6. The Best Thing About the Character

_____

_____

_____

_____

3. Something the Character Says

4. A Problem the Character Has

Ready-to-Use Independent Reading Management Kit   Scholastic Professional Books

Level 7

Name _____ Date _____

Book Title _____

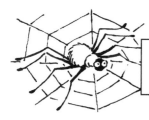

My Book Poem

Write a poem about your book.
Here are some things you can include:

✔ characters

✔ setting

✔ events

✔ why you like the book

Share your poem with a friend.

Name _____ Date _____

Book Title _____

Adjectives From A to Z

Look for adjectives in your book.
Try to find an adjective that begins with each letter.
(If you can't find adjectives for every letter, look in
a dictionary or think of some on your own.)
Write them on the lines.

A _____   N _____

B _____   O _____

C _____   P _____

D _____   Q _____

E _____   R _____

F _____   S _____

G _____   T _____

H _____   U _____

I _____   V _____

J _____   W _____

K _____   X _____

L _____   Y _____

M _____   Z _____

Level 7

Name _____ Date _____

Book Title _____

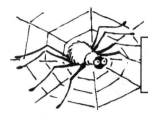

Verb Endings

Find verbs with the endings *-ing* and *-ed*.
Write a verb on each line.
Underline each base word and circle the ending.

-ing	-ed
<u>snorkel</u>(ing)	<u>jump</u>(ed)

Ready-to-Use Independent Reading Management Kit Scholastic Professional Books

Level 7

Name _____   Date _____

Book Title _____

Antonym Ants

Find 4 words in your book.
Write each word in one segment of an ant.
Then write an antonym for each word in
the other segment of the ant.

top bottom

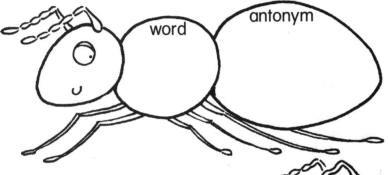

word   antonym

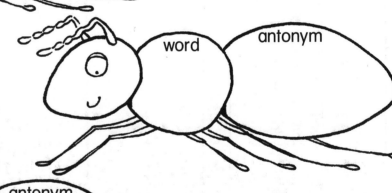

word   antonym

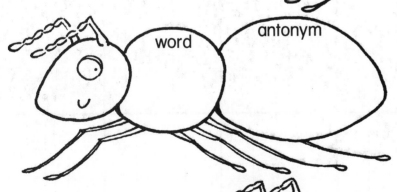

word   antonym

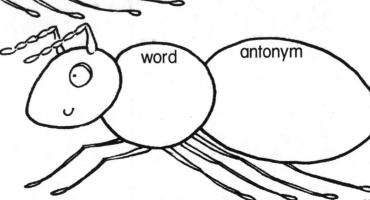

word   antonym

Level 7

Name _____ Date _____

Book Title _____

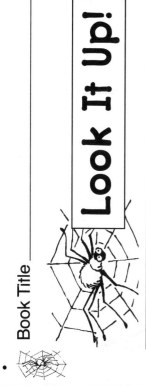

Look It Up!

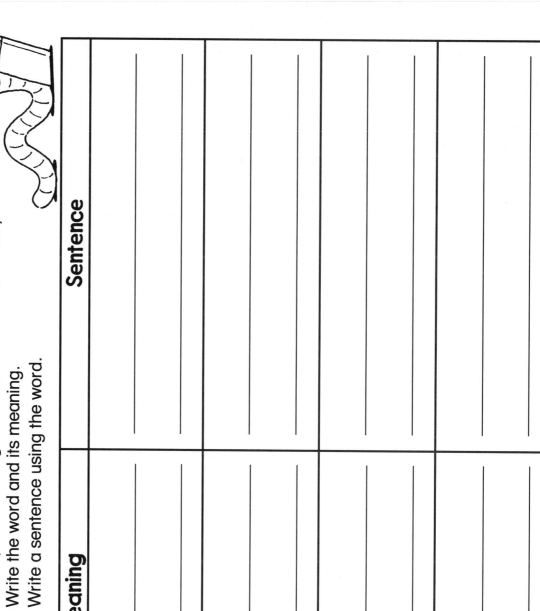

In your book, find 4 words whose meanings you do not know.
Look up the meaning of each word in the dictionary.
Write the word and its meaning.
Write a sentence using the word.

Word	Meaning	Sentence
1.		
2.		
3.		
4.		

Name _____ Date _____

Make a Mini-Book

On each page, write something important that happens in your book.

Draw a picture on each page. Cut out and fold your mini-book.

✂

Next,

Then,

- - - - - - - - Fold along dotted line. - - - - - - - -

Fold along dotted line.

Book Title _____

_____

Last, _____

First, _____

Ready-to-Use Independent Reading Management Kit   Scholastic Professional Books

Level 7

Name _____ Date _____

Book Title _____

Character Puppet

Make a puppet of a character in your book.

Draw the character in the outline.

Add details and color the puppet.

Cut out the character.

Glue the character to a popsicle stick.

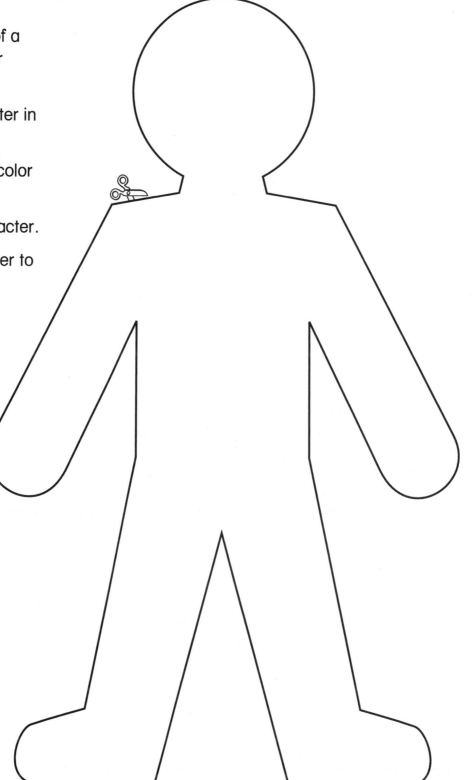

Ready-to-Use Independent Reading Management Kit   Scholastic Professional Books

Level 7 • Art

Level 7

Name _____   Date _____

Independent Reading Contract

Book Title: _____

This book was: ☐ **easy**   ☐ **just right**   ☐ **challenging**

Complete the activities based on your independent reading book.
When you have finished an activity, color in the box on the chart.

Activities marked with a star ✻ have an activity sheet.

Reading	Writing	Skills	Art
(Choose _____)	(Choose _____)	(Choose _____)	(Choose _____)
Read to yourself.	✻ Fill in a character tree.	✻ Write quotations from your book.	✻ Make a story quilt.
Read to a classmate whose first name starts with the same letter as yours.	✻ Write your opinion about the book.	✻ Fill in prefix clouds with words and their prefixes.	✻ Draw character cards.
Read to a family member.	✻ Write character riddles.	✻ Find 4 proper nouns.	Use clay to create a setting from your book.
Read an exciting part of your book to your teacher.	✻ Describe the main character with proof from the story.	✻ Find 4 fabulous words and use them in sentences.	Draw an exciting scene from your book and write a caption for it.

Nancy
girl

Ready-to-Use Independent Reading Management Kit   Scholastic Professional Books

Level 8

Name _____

Date _____

Book Title _____

Character Tree

Fill in the tree to tell about a character in your book.

1. name of the character

_____

2. two words about the character

_____

3. three words about what the character wants

_____

4. four words about how the character grows or changes

_____

5. five words about how the character reaches a goal

_____

Level 8 · Writing

Ready-to-Use Independent Reading Management Kit Scholastic Professional Books

Name _____ Date _____

Book Title _____

My Opinion

Use the form to tell what you think about your book.

I think this book is: ☐ poor ☐ good ☐ very good ☐ excellent

My favorite part of the book is _____

_____

_____

I like this part because _____

_____

_____

The main character reminds me of _____

_____

_____

I think the author is good at _____

_____

_____

I would recommend this book to a friend. ☐ yes ☐ no ☐ maybe

Level 8

Name _____ Date _____

Book Title _____

Character Riddles

Write riddles about some characters in your book.

Find a classmate who has read your book and share your riddles.

Note: Riddles do not have to rhyme.

Example:

**We build houses pretty fast.
Two of our houses do not last.
Who are we?**

Riddle 1 _____

Riddle 2 _____

Ready-to-Use Independent Reading Management Kit   Scholastic Professional Books

Level 8

Name _____ Date _____

Book Title _____

Describe the Main Character

Draw the main character in your book.
Make a list of words to describe the character.
Write the part in the book that backs up your
description of the character.

Words to Describe the Character

_____

_____

_____

_____

_____

_____

_____

_____

_____

_____

_____

_____

Character's Name

_____

_____

Proof From the Book _____

_____

_____

_____

_____

_____

Name _____   Date _____

Book Title _____

Look Who's Talking

In each speech balloon, write an important
quotation from a character in your book.
Draw the character who says each one.

Quotation

Character:

Quotation

Character:

Quotation

Character:

Ready-to-Use Independent Reading Management Kit   Scholastic Professional Books

Level 8

Name _____ Date _____

Book Title _____

 **Prefix Clouds**

In your book, find words with prefixes.
Write the prefix in the first cloud segment.
Write the word in the second cloud segment.

(mid) (night)

Level 8

Name _____ Date _____

Book Title _____

Proper Noun Tea Party

Find 4 proper nouns in your book.
In each teacup, write a proper noun.
In the saucer, write the common noun
for each proper noun.

Nancy
girl

1.

Proper Noun

Common Noun

2.

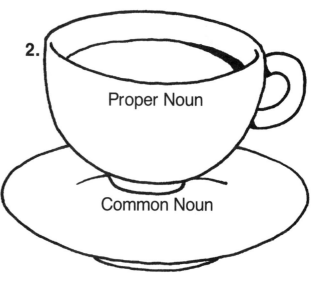

Proper Noun

Common Noun

3.

Proper Noun

Common Noun

4.

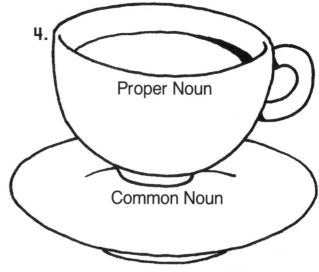

Proper Noun

Common Noun

Ready-to-Use Independent Reading Management Kit   Scholastic Professional Books

Level 8

Name _____ Date _____

Book Title _____

 Four Fabulous Words

Look for 4 fabulous words in your book.
Write them on the lines.
Use each word in your own sentence.

Fabulous Word

1. _____

   _____

2. _____

   _____

3. _____

   _____

4. _____

   _____

Sentence

_____

_____

_____

_____
_____

_____

_____

_____

_____

_____

_____

_____

Ready-to-Use Independent Reading Management Kit Scholastic Professional Books

Name _____ Date _____

Book Title _____

 Story Quilt

Fill in the story quilt.

In each square, draw a picture of someone or
something important in your story.

Use your quilt to retell the story to a classmate.

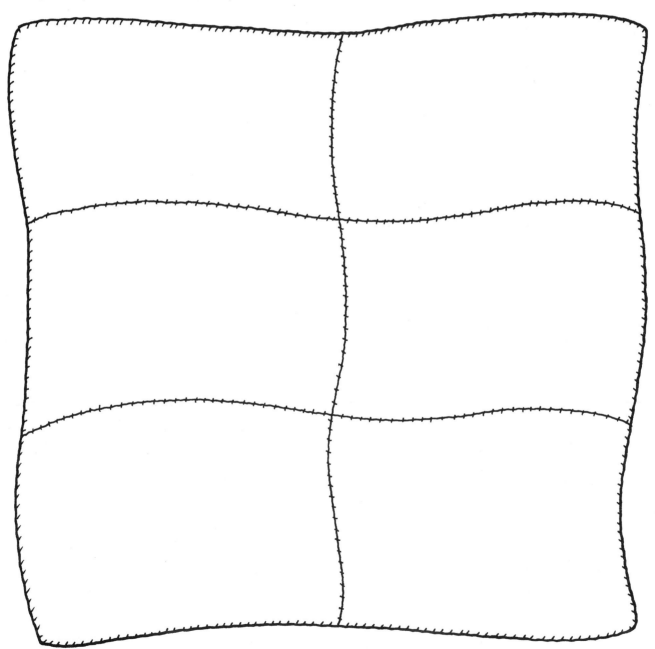

Ready-to-Use Independent Reading Management Kit   Scholastic Professional Books

Level 8

Name _____ Date _____

Book Title _____

Character Cards

Choose 4 important characters from your book.
Draw a picture of one character on each card.
Write important information about each character.

Character's Name _____ **Important Information** _____ _____ _____	**Character's Name** _____ **Important Information** _____ _____ _____
Character's Name _____ **Important Information** _____ _____ _____	**Character's Name** _____ **Important Information** _____ _____ _____

Ready-to-Use Independent Reading Management Kit   Scholastic Professional Books

Level 8

Name _____ Date _____

Independent Reading Contract

Book Title: _____

This book was: ☐ **easy** ☐ **just right** ☐ **challenging**

Complete the activities based on your independent reading book.
When you have finished an activity, color in the box on the chart.

Activities marked with a star ✱ have an activity sheet.

Reading (Choose ____)	Writing (Choose ____)	Skills (Choose ____)	Art (Choose ____)
Read to yourself.	✱Complete a reader response form.	✱Compare yourself to a character, using a Venn diagram.	✱Make a comic strip.
Read to someone in a lower grade.	✱Write an introduction to your book.	✱Go on a homonym hunt.	✱Make a picture dictionary using words from your book.
Read to a friend.	✱Write a newspaper article about your book.	✱Find 4 action verbs and write sentences using them.	Draw a poster for your book. Hang it in the library to advertise your book.
Read a description of a character to your teacher.	✱Write a letter of advice to a character.	✱Go on an apostrophe search.	Make a diorama of a place in your book.
	✱Create an outline for a sequel to your book.	✱Write a dialogue using quotation marks. " "	Draw a map to show the main setting in your book.

Name _____ Date _____

Book Title _____

Reader Response

Answer the questions below in complete sentences.

1. What is your favorite part of the book? Why?

_____

_____

_____

_____

2. Are there parts you don't like? What are they?

_____

_____

_____

_____

3. Write your favorite sentence.

_____

_____

4. Who is your favorite character in this book? Why?

_____

_____

_____

_____

5. What did you learn from this book?

_____

_____

_____

_____

Name _____ Date _____

Book Title _____

A Book Introduction

Pretend you are going to introduce
your book to the class.
What will you say about it?
Write an introduction.
Include the things on the list.

✔ book title
✔ author
✔ illustrator
✔ setting
✔ important characters
✔ short summary
✔ a highlight (funny part, exciting part, favorite part)
✔ why others might want to read it

Ready-to-Use Independent Reading Management Kit   Scholastic Professional Books

Name _____ Date _____

Book Title _____

"Extra! Extra!"

Write a newspaper article
about your book.
Include a picture.

Name of newspaper

Date

Headline

Article

Picture

Caption

Level 9

Name _____   Date _____

Book Title _____

Advice for a Character

Most characters have a problem.
Write a letter to a character in your book.
In the letter, give your character advice
about a problem he or she is having.

Dear _____,

_____

_____

_____

_____

_____

_____

_____

Sincerely, _____

_____

_____

Ready-to-Use Independent Reading Management Kit   Scholastic Professional Books

Level 9

Name _____ Date _____

Book Title _____

Plan a Sequel

Help the author plan a sequel to the book.
Complete the outline with your ideas.

I. Characters

A. _____

B. _____

C. _____

II. Settings

A. _____

B. _____

C. _____

III. Exciting Events

A. _____

B. _____

C. _____

IV. Ending

A. _____

B. _____

Ready-to-Use Independent Reading Management Kit   Scholastic Professional Books

Level 9

Name _____ Date _____

Book Title _____

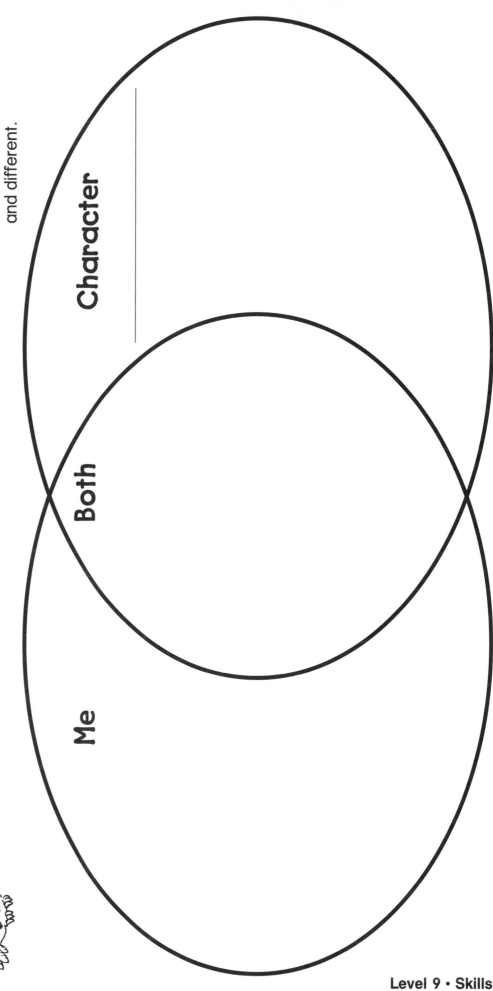

Compare Yourself to a Character

How are you like a character in your book? Fill in the Venn diagram to show how you are similar and different.

Character

Both

Me

Ready-to-Use Independent Reading Management Kit   Scholastic Professional Books

Name _____   Date _____

Book Title _____

Homonym Hunt

A homonym is a word that sounds the
same as another word but has a different
spelling and meaning.
Find homonyms in your book.
Write other homonyms for each word.
One is done for you.

Homonyms in My Book	Other Homonyms
to	too, two

Ready-to-Use Independent Reading Management Kit   Scholastic Professional Books

Level 9

Name _____ Date _____

Book Title _____

Action Verbs

In your book, find 4 verbs that show
interesting actions.
Use each verb in your own sentence.

flutter
Glide

Verb

1. _____

_____

2. _____

_____

3. _____

_____

4. _____

_____

Sentence

_____

_____

_____

_____

_____

_____

_____

_____

_____

_____

_____

_____

_____

_____

_____

_____

Ready-to-Use Independent Reading Management Kit Scholastic Professional Books

Level 9

Name _____ Date _____

Book Title _____

Apostrophe Search

In your book, find 10 words with apostrophes.

They can be used in contractions, such as **it's** or **they're**.

They can be used to show possession, such as **Charlie's** fish
or **cats'** tails.

In the chart below, write words with apostrophes.

Contractions	Possession
it's	Sarah's

Level 9

Name _____   Date _____

Book Title _____

Write a Dialogue

Choose 2 characters from your book.
Make up a short dialogue that they might have.
Write the dialogue, using quotation marks.

For example:

"Hello, Fred. Where are you going?"
asked Rhonda.
"I'm going fishing. Would you like
to come?" said Fred.
"Sure! That sounds like fun!" said Rhonda.

_____
_____
_____
_____
_____
_____
_____
_____
_____
_____
_____
_____
_____

Ready-to-Use Independent Reading Management Kit   Scholastic Professional Books

Name _____   Date _____

Book Title _____

Cartoon Time

Make a comic strip based on the book.
In each panel, draw pictures about the book.
Add speech balloons.
Color the pictures.

Picture Dictionary

Choose 5 words from your book.
Write each word on one page of the
mini-book below.
Draw a picture to show the word's meaning.

Cut out the dictionary pages.
Arrange the pages in ABC order.
Staple them together to make a book.

's

Picture
Dictionary

Ready-to-Use Independent Reading Management Kit   Scholastic Professional Books

Level 9

Name _____   Date _____

Independent Reading Contract

Book Title: _____

This book was: ☐ easy   ☐ just right   ☐ challenging

Complete the activities based on your independent reading book.
When you have finished an activity, color in the box on the chart.

Activities marked with a star ✱ have an activity sheet.

Reading (Choose _____)	Writing (Choose _____)	Skills (Choose _____)	Art (Choose _____)
Read to yourself.	✱ Write a book review.	✱ Go on an adverb search.	✱ Make a jigsaw puzzle based on your book.
Read to a student in a lower grade.	✱ Fill out a report card for a character. A+ B− C+	✱ Find and sort nouns, adjectives, and verbs.	✱ Draw a character's favorite things.
Read to someone at home.	✱ Write an acrostic poem about a character.	✱ Complete a word web.	✱ Design a travel brochure about the setting of your book.
Read to a classmate.	✱ Write questions to ask the author. ? ? ? ? ?	✱ Fill in a pronoun chart.	Make a diorama of a scene from your book.
Read an important part to your teacher.	✱ Make a story pyramid.	✱ Design a character name search.	Retell your story in pictures.

Level 10

Name _____ Date _____

Book Review

Fill out the review form.
Share your review with classmates.

Book Title _____

Author _____

Book Rating (Circle one.)   poor   1   2   3   4   5   great

This is what I liked about the book: _____

_____

_____

_____

This is what I did not like about the book: _____

_____

_____

I would recommend this book because _____

_____

_____

_____

OR

I would not recommend this book because _____

_____

_____

Ready-to-Use Independent Reading Management Kit   Scholastic Professional Books

Name _____ Date _____

Book Title _____

Grade a Character

Characters often have strong points and weak points.
Choose a character from your book.
Give the character a grade for each category.
Explain why you gave the character those grades.

Character's name _____

Category	Grade	Comments
Responsibility		
Thoughtfulness		
Friendship		
Generosity		
Sense of humor		
Problem solving		

Acrostic Poem

Write the letters of the main character's name
in the boxes down the left side of the page.
Next to each letter, write a word or phrase
that starts with that letter.
The word should describe the character.

S mart
A thletic
M ouse

Ready-to-Use Independent Reading Management Kit   Scholastic Professional Books

Level 10

Name _____ Date _____

Book Title _____

Author Interview

If you could meet the author of your book,
what questions would you ask?
Write 5 questions for the author.
You can ask about the author, the book, the
writing process, or other topics of interest.

Author _____

1. _____

_____

2. _____

_____

3. _____

_____

4. _____

_____

_____

5. _____

_____

_____

Name _____   Date _____

Book Title _____

Story Pyramid

Make a story pyramid about your book.

Title

Characters

Setting

Important Events

1. _____

2. _____

3. _____

Ending

Ready-to-Use Independent Reading Management Kit   Scholastic Professional Books

Level 10

Name _____ Date _____

Book Title _____

Find 5 adverbs in your book.
Use each adverb in a sentence.
Underline the adverbs.

slowly

1. _____
_____
_____

2. _____
_____
_____

3. _____
_____
_____

4. _____
_____
_____
_____

5. _____
_____
_____
_____

Ready-to-Use Independent Reading Management Kit   Scholastic Professional Books

Level 10

Name _____   Date _____

Book Title _____

 **Find & Sort**

Find 5 nouns, 5 adjectives, and 5 verbs in
your book.
Write them in the correct place on the chart.

Nouns	Adjectives	Verbs
television	sharp	kick
1. _____	1. _____	1. _____
2. _____	2. _____	2. _____
3. _____	3. _____	3. _____
4. _____	4. _____	4. _____
5. _____	5. _____	5. _____

Ready-to-Use Independent Reading Management Kit   Scholastic Professional Books

Name _____

Date _____

Book Title _____

Word Web

Find a new word in your book.
Write the word in the top circle.
Fill in the web.

(Word)

Sentence from book with word

My own sentence with word

Dictionary meaning

★Bonus★

Find 2 other new words in your book. Make a word web for each on another sheet of paper.

Name _____

Date _____

Book Title _____

Pronoun Picnic

Find 5 pronouns in your book.
Write the sentence in which you found each pronoun.
Underline the pronoun.
Tell who or what each pronoun stands for.

	Pronoun in a sentence	Word that pronoun refers to
Example	<u>It</u> was sweet and juicy.	watermelon
1.		
2.		
3.		
4.		
5.		

Ready-to-Use Independent Reading Management Kit Scholastic Professional Books

Level 10 • Skills

Name _____ Date _____

Book Title _____

Character Name Search

Name Search

Choose 5 characters from your book.

Write their names in the grid, going either across or down.

Add other letters to the grid to hide the names.

Write a clue for each character.

Have a classmate who has read your book find and circle the names.

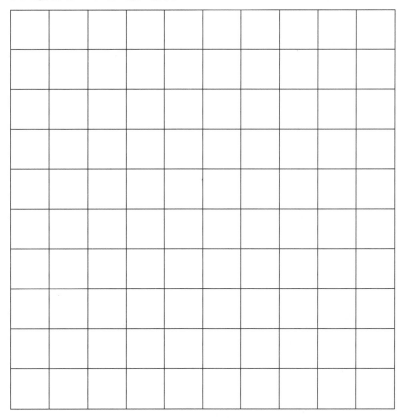

Clues

1. _____

2. _____

3. _____

4. _____

5. _____

Ready-to-Use Independent Reading Management Kit   Scholastic Professional Books

Name _____ Date _____

Book Title _____

Draw a picture of a person or place from your book.
Color the picture with crayons.
Cut out the puzzle pieces.
Invite a friend to put together your puzzle.

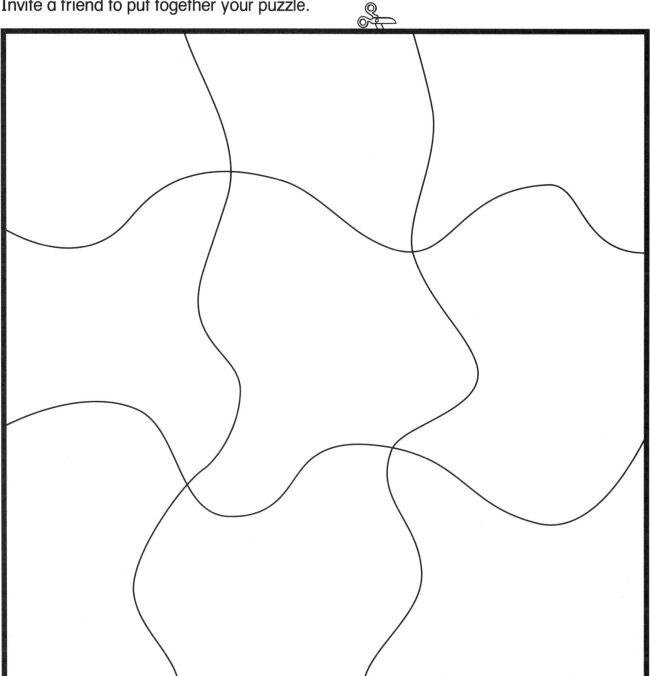

Ready-to-Use Independent Reading Management Kit   Scholastic Professional Books

Level 10

Name _____ Date _____

Book Title _____

Favorite Things

Choose a character from your book.
On the shelf, draw pictures of some
of your character's favorite things.

_____'s Shelf

Travel Brochure

Design a travel brochure about the setting of your book.
Show visitors all the great places to go!
Cut out the brochure and fold along the dotted lines.
Draw or paste pictures from magazines on both sides of
the brochure. Write about the places.

Ready-to-Use Independent Reading Management Kit   Scholastic Professional Books

Level 10 • Art

Name _____   Date _____

Books I've Read

Date Finished	Title	Author
1.		
2.		
3.		
4.		
5.		
6.		
7.		
8.		
9.		
10.		
11.		
12.		
13.		

Name _____ Date _____

Check-Out Form for Level _____

I'm ready to check out my Independent Reading Contract.

- ☐ I completed the right number of activities.
- ☐ I did my best work.
- ☐ I shared my work with a classmate.
- ☐ I stapled my pages in order.
- ☐ I wrote the date, title, and author in my Independent Reading Contract folder.

Name _____ Date _____

Check-Out Form for Level _____

I'm ready to check out my Independent Reading Contract.

- ☐ I completed the right number of activities.
- ☐ I did my best work.
- ☐ I shared my work with a classmate.
- ☐ I stapled my pages in order.
- ☐ I wrote the date, title, and author in my Independent Reading Contract folder.

Ready-to-Use Independent Reading Management Kit   Scholastic Professional Books

Name _____ Date _____

Self-Assessment Rubric for Level ____

	1 Point	2 Points	3 Points	Score
NEATNESS	Most of my work is not neat.	Most of my work is neat.	All of my work is neat.	
WORK	I could have done a better job on my work.	I did a good job on my work.	I did my very best work!	
TIME	I took too long to finish my work.	I finished my work on time.	I finished sooner than was expected of me.	

Total Score _____

Name _____ Date _____

Self-Assessment Rubric for Level ____

	1 Point	2 Points	3 Points	Score
NEATNESS	Most of my work is not neat.	Most of my work is neat.	All of my work is neat.	
WORK	I could have done a better job on my work.	I did a good job on my work.	I did my very best work!	
TIME	I took too long to finish my work.	I finished my work on time.	I finished sooner than was expected of me.	

Total Score _____

Teacher Record

Student _____

Independent Reading Contract Level _____ Date _____

Book Title and Author: _____

_____

Reading Level: _____

Rubric Score: _____

Comments: _____

_____

Independent Reading Contract Level _____ Date _____

Book Title and Author: _____

_____

Reading Level: _____

Rubric Score: _____

Comments: _____

_____

Independent Reading Contract Level _____ Date _____

Book Title and Author: _____

_____

Reading Level: _____

Rubric Score: _____

Comments: _____

_____

Ready-to-Use Independent Reading Management Kit   Scholastic Professional Books

Letter Home

Dear _____,

Throughout the year, the students in my class will be reading books of their own choice. To help children get the most out of their books, our reading program features independent reading contracts. Each contract offers a variety of activities that encourage students to respond to literature in meaningful ways. The activities include reading comprehension, writing, vocabulary, grammar, punctuation, phonics, art, and more. Children make choices about which activities they will complete. A popular choice is to read to someone at home. I hope that you will enjoy helping your child fulfill this important part of the assignment.

When children master the skills on one contract, we will move on to another contract with new and more advanced skills. Before we begin a new contract, I will teach the skills necessary to complete it. Children will meet with me when they have finished a contract to talk about both the book they have read and the activities they have completed.

In addition to building important language arts skills, independent reading contracts also help students learn to work independently and purposefully. Although there is a wide variety of activities in the contracts, the structure and procedures are consistent. This allows children to work on their own while I am meeting with individuals or small groups of students.

The goal of our independent reading program is to foster a love of reading and to help children build important reading and writing skills. I look forward to helping each student reach this goal. Please feel free to call me if you have questions.

Sincerely,

_____

Name _____ Date _____

Independent Reading Contract

Book Title: _____

This book was: ☐ easy ☐ just right ☐ challenging

Complete the activities based on your independent reading book.
When you have finished an activity, color in the box on the chart.

Reading	Writing	Skills	Art
(Choose _____)	(Choose _____)	(Choose _____)	(Choose _____)

Ready-to-Use Independent Reading Management Kit   Scholastic Professional Books